7/09

Energy

Tim Clifford

Rourke
Publishing LLC
Vero Beach, Florida 32964

www.rourkepublishing.com

PHOTO CREDITS: Title Page: © Mark Stout; page 4: © Peter Finnie; page 5: © Groelsfse; page 6: © Tom Marvin; page 7,8: © Tony Tromblay, Bjorn Kindler; page 10: © Sami Suni, David Philips; page 11: © Jeff Dalton; page 12: © Lou Oates; page 13: © Nancy Louie; page 15: © Michelle Cottrill; page 16: © Peter McKinnon; page 17: © Matt Matthews; page 18: © Daniel Rodriguez, Mario Tarello; page 19: Lee, James Steidl; page 21: © Edward Todd; page 22: © Michael utech; page 23: © Pawel Marksum; page 24: © George Argyropoulos; page 25: © Narvikk; page 29: ©Douglas Freer, Daniel Stein; page 30: © Andrew Penner; page 31: © Malcolm Romain; page 32: © Alex Yurchenko; page 33: © Alexander Hafemann; page 34: Jeff Strickler; page 35: Rob Hill; page 36: Soubrette; page 37: James Ferrie; page 38: David H. Lewis; page 40: René Mansi; page 41: Pattie Calfy; page 43: Otmar Smit; page 44: Richard Foreman.

Editor: Robert Stengard-Olliges

Cover design by Nicky Stratford, bdpublishing.com

Interior Design by Renee Brady

Library of Congress Cataloging-in-Publication Data

Printed in the USA

CG/CG

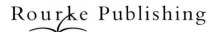

Rourke Publishing

www.rourkepublishing.com – rourke@rourkepublishing.com
Post Office Box 3328. Vero Beach. FL 32964

CONTENTS

CHAPTER ONE

WHAT IS ENERGY?

You need energy to work.

Have you ever woken up very tired in the morning, unable even to lift your head from the pillow? If so, it's likely that you said to yourself, "I have no **energy** today!" Of course, you had some energy, or you wouldn't even be able to open your eyes!

What you probably meant was that you didn't have enough energy to do something, like get out of bed and go to school. Energy can be defined as the ability to do **work**.

Work is the ability to make an object move in some way. Electricity moves through wires to light up a bulb. Your alarm clock uses electrical energy to make the sound that wakes you up. The energy of the wind causes your curtains to wave gently.

Looking out the window, you may see cars burning fuel as energy to zoom down the street. If something is moving, or doing work, it is using energy.

Electricity lighting up a light bulb.

CHAPTER TWO

HOW WE USE ENERGY

Energy is used to light up this house.

There are three main ways we use energy. We use it to travel, to manufacture goods, and in our homes and businesses. Which of these three uses the most energy? You might be surprised at the answer!

Energy Use in Transportation

Motor vehicles are everywhere. There are over 240 million motor vehicles in the United States alone! All of them need energy to run. Think of all the energy they must use! Yet, even if you added in all the airplanes, trains, and boats, transportation still comes in third in energy use. About 28 percent of the energy in the United States is used for transportation.

Vehicles use a lot of energy.

Airplanes use a lot of energy.

Energy Use in Industry

Almost every item you buy is manufactured. The manufacturing process uses tremendous amounts of energy. Energy is used to find or create new materials to make the goods we buy. These materials must be heated, cooled, molded into shapes, and assembled. Even the cooked foods you buy in the supermarket used energy in the cooking process. Making all the items you can buy, eat, or wear uses only 32 percent of our energy.

This manufacturing plant uses energy.

Energy Use in Homes and Buildings

Homes and commercial buildings use more energy than either industry or transportation.

The homes we live in use energy to keep people warm in the winter and cool in the summer. All our appliances, from TV sets to microwave ovens, use energy.

Commercial buildings include places where people work but usually don't live. These include buildings such as your school, stores, hospitals, post offices, and many other types of buildings.

Think of all the different ways your home and school use energy. Now you can see why homes and commercial buildings use 40 percent of our energy, more than manufacturing or transportation.

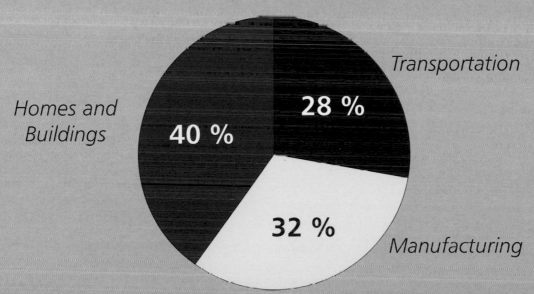

Percentage of Energy Use

Transportation

Homes and Buildings

28 %

40 %

32 %

Manufacturing

CHAPTER THREE

KINETIC VS. POTENTIAL ENERGY

There are two types of energy, called kinetic and potential. **Kinetic energy** is the energy of movement. **Potential energy** is stored energy.

Skiing is a form of kinetic energy.

Batteries are potential energy.

Kinetic Energy

Think of a ballerina leaping through the air, or a baseball pitcher throwing a fastball. These involve movement, so they are examples of kinetic energy. Objects can also have kinetic energy. The movement of the pitcher's arm gives kinetic energy to the baseball. In fact, any object that is in motion has kinetic energy.

In order to have motion, energy must be transferred from one object to another. When you write with a pencil, you are transferring energy from your hand to the pencil to make it move. Can you think of other examples of kinetic Energy?

A rollercoaster is kinetic energy.

Potential Energy

When someone tells you that you have potential, they are telling you that you have the ability to do something in the future. Potential energy is the same thing—it has the ability to become kinetic energy.

The boulder hitting this car is potential energy that changed to kinetic energy.

That ability may come from gravity. A boulder sitting on top of a mountain has potential energy, because if it begins to roll down the mountain it will gain kinetic energy as gravity pulls it to the Earth. The higher the boulder is, the more potential energy it contains.

Another type of potential energy is elastic. When you pull on a rubber band, it stretches and gains potential energy. It is not moving yet, but when you let it go, it will sail through the air. How far it will go depends on how tightly you stretch it. The more it is stretched, the more potential energy it has and the further it will travel when you let it go.

Potential energy can also be released by a chemical or nuclear reaction.

This slingshot has potential energy.

CHAPTER FOUR

FORMS OF ENERGY

While there are only two types of energy, kinetic and potential, there are many more forms of energy. Some of these forms are kinetic and some are potential.

Some of the forms of kinetic energy we will examine in this book are **heat** (thermal), radiant, and electrical. The forms of potential energy we will look at are chemical and nuclear.

Tea kettles are a form of heat energy.

Car batteries are electrical energy.

Heat Energy

Heat energy is the movement of energy from one object to another. It is also called thermal energy. It can move in three ways: through conduction, convection, or radiation.

Hot vehicles in the summer are a form of heat energy.

Conduction occurs when heat moves directly from one object to another. What happens when you leave your car parked in a sunny parking lot on a hot day? The heat of the sun passes directly through the metal of the car and heats the air (and seats) on the inside.

Convection is the movement of hot liquids or gases. For example, when you boil water, the liquid nearest the flame heats up first. As it gets hot, it rises, and the cooler water goes to the bottom where it gets heated. This continues until the water is boiled.

Radiation is the movement of energy in the form of waves. Turn the page for more information on radiant energy.

Boiling water is heat energy.

Radiant Energy

Radiant energy is the energy created through electromagnetic waves, such as light, heat, or radio waves. The sun is our major source of radiant energy because it gives off a great amount of heat and light. Scientists use the electromagnetic spectrum to discuss the types of radiant energy. The electromagnetic spectrum lists all the types of radiant energy by the length of their waves. The shorter the wave, the more energy and heat are created.

Electromagnetic Spectrum

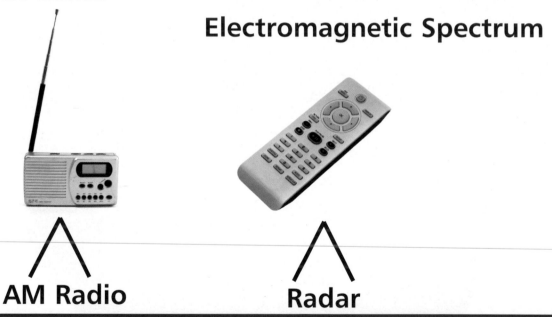

AM Radio   **Radar**

| 0 | 10^2 | 10^4 | 10^6 | 10^8 | 10^{10} |

Frequency in hertz (hz)

Most radiant energy can't be seen, but there is a small part of the electromagnetic spectrum that is called visible light. This is the light we can see. Differences in the length of the waves in this part of the spectrum cause us to see different colors.

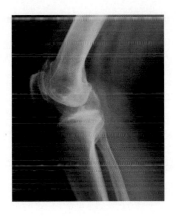

Visible Light

X-Ray

10^{12} 10^{14} 10^{16} 10^{18} 10^{20} 10^{22}

Electrical Energy

A huge maze of wires in every house carries electrical energy to do many different jobs, from lighting your home to cooking food.

Electricity starts at the atomic level. Atoms are made up of a nucleus, protons, and electrons. We create electricity by forcing electrons to move from atom to atom. **Electrical energy** is the movement of electrons through a conductor. A conductor is a material that can carry electricity, like the wiring in homes.

Generators create the electricity used in our everyday lives, but other forms of electric energy occur naturally.

Lightning occurs when electrons are discharged from a cloud. Lightning is so powerful that if we could capture the electricity in a single bolt, it could power our entire home for days.

Static Electricity occurs when an object (or person) gets charged with electrons. You may have experienced this when scuffing your feet on a carpet and then touching a doorknob. The electrons you built up jump from your hand to the metal of the doorknob, causing a powerful shock!

A man checking the electricity meter.

Chemical Energy

Chemicals contain stored, or potential, energy to hold their atoms together. When chemicals are mixed together, a reaction can occur. **Chemical energy** is the energy released through a chemical reaction.

We can use the heat that these reactions give off. We can use it to cook, to heat our homes, and to burn the gasoline that moves our cars.

One of the major uses of chemical energy is to help produce electrical energy. Coal, gas, and other fuels are burned to run electric generators.

The chemical energy in batteries is changed into the electrical energy we need to run everything from flashlights to toys.

A coal plant.

Chemical energy batteries power this flashlight.

Nuclear Energy

Atoms are so small that until recently even the most powerful microscopes could not see them. Yet when we split the nucleus of an atom, a tremendous amount of energy is released. **Nuclear energy** is the potential energy stored in the nucleus of an atom.

In a nuclear power plant, a reactor is used to split uranium atoms. This heat is used to turn water to steam. The steam powers a generator that creates electricity.

Nuclear power plants create about 20 percent of the electricity in the United States. Coal, oil, and natural gas help produce the rest.

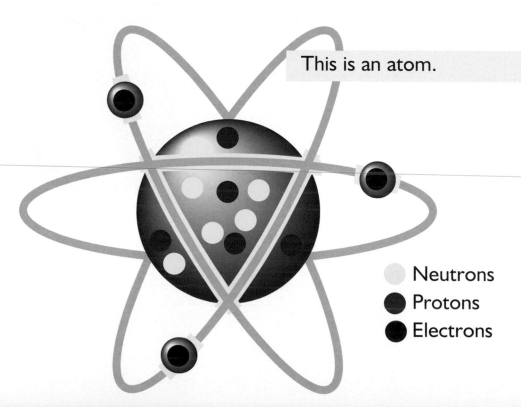

This is an atom.

○ Neutrons
● Protons
● Electrons

Cooling towers at a nuclear power plant.

CHAPTER FIVE

CONSERVATION AND TRANSFORMATION OF ENERGY

When you think of energy conservation, you probably think of ways to save energy in your home. When scientists speak of the **Law of Conservation of Energy**, they mean something very different.

This law states that energy can neither be created nor destroyed. In other words, the amount of energy that exists remains the same, but it is often changed from one type into another.

Think of that day when you woke up without any energy. Eating breakfast helped get you moving. The potential chemical energy in the food you ate was changed into the kinetic energy that got you up and moving.

Here are some examples of how energy is changed from one type to another.

- *The radiant energy of the sun becomes the chemical energy stored in food*

- *The chemical energy in food becomes the energy your body needs to do work*

- *The nuclear energy in an atom becomes electrical energy in a reactor*

- *Electrical energy in your home becomes thermal energy in a heater*

- *The chemical energy in gasoline becomes the motion energy of your car*

CHAPTER SIX

RENEWABLE VS. NON-RENEWABLE ENERGY

A century ago, before there were so many electrical appliances and automobiles, we didn't need to produce much energy. Today, just about everything we use needs some form of energy. To meet the high energy requirements of all the things we need and want to do, we must produce energy from many sources.

These sources are either **renewable** or **non-renewable**.

Using trees for energy.

Renewable energy is energy that can be used over and over, without running out. Non-renewable energy is energy that we will run out of someday.

Non-Renewable Energy Sources

In the United States, most of our energy comes from non-renewable sources. Of these, the main types are fossil fuels, propane, and uranium. Each of these presents problems. Uranium is dangerous to humans and difficult to store. Fossil fuels (coal, oil, and natural gas) and propane are burned, so they create pollution. The sulfur dioxide from burning coal creates acid rain. Fossil fuels also give off carbon dioxide, which many scientists believe adds to the greenhouse effect and global warming.

Acid Rain

Greenhouse Effect

Acid Rain: When rain becomes acidic, it can pollute lakes and streams, harming the animals that live there. It can also cause damage to forests and even cause buildings to decay over time.

Greenhouse Effect: Many scientists believe that carbon dioxide and other gases in the air can trap energy in the Earth's atmosphere, causing the Earth to get warmer. This contributes to global warming, or an increase in the average temperature of the Earth. This can have harmful effects on the world's oceans, weather, and animal life.

The largest category of non-renewable energy is **fossil fuels**, which are fuels that come from dead organisms, such as plants and animals that died many millions of years ago. There are three main types: coal is a solid, oil is a liquid, and natural gas is a gas.

Type of fossil fuel	How it is produced
Coal	Mined from the ground
Oil (petroleum)	Pulled from Earth by oil wells
Natural Gas	Pulled from Earth by gas wells

All of these fossil fuels are burned. When we burn them, they give us energy to create electricity, heat our houses, and power our vehicles.

Oil Rig.

Uranium is a non-renewable energy source. It is used in the process of creating nuclear energy. It is non-renewable because there is only a small amount of uranium in the world.

Propane is created during natural gas and oil production. It is a gas, but it can be made into a liquid to make it easier to transport. Because it comes from two other non-renewable sources, propane itself is non-renewable.

Trucks hauling coal from a strip mine.

Renewable Energy Sources

Renewable energy sources have some advantages over non-renewable sources. Most important, we can use renewable sources again and again without running out. In addition, renewable sources usually create a lot less pollution.

There are some disadvantages to renewable energy as well. It can be difficult to harness, or gain control over. Some forms can be very expensive to use. Some depend on the weather, so they can be undependable. Finally, it can be difficult to generate enough energy using these sources to meet our growing energy demands.

Hoover Dam.

Solar energy is energy that comes from the sun. The radiation of the sun is captured in solar panels that are exposed to sunlight. The sunlight can be changed into electrical energy to power all the appliances in a home. It can also be used to heat a house and to create hot water. The main problems with solar energy are that the panels take up a lot of space and energy collection depends on the weather.

Hydropower is energy captured from the movement of water. It is sometimes called hydroelectric power because the water is used to turn turbines that create electricity. While hydropower creates almost no pollution, it can cause changes to the environment that affect animals and plants.

Solar panels conduct energy from the sun.

Wind power is energy captured from the movement of the wind. The most familiar form of wind power is the windmill, which uses the wind's energy to grind grain. More common today is the wind **turbine**. Like a windmill, its blades are turned by the wind, which spins a turbine that generates electricity. Wind is a very clean source of power, but it requires large, sometimes noisy blades to operate.

Geothermal energy is energy that comes from the Earth in the form of water or steam. The Earth's interior is extremely hot—hot enough to melt the rock that comes out of a volcano in the form of lava. That heat creates hot water and steam below the Earth's surface, which can be harnessed by digging a well. As the steam or water rises, it can be used to run a turbine and create electricity.

These modern day windmills conduct energy from the wind.

Biomass energy is plant material and animal waste burned as fuel. Biomass comes from recently living organisms, not the million-year-old materials that form fossil fuels.

Wood is a major source of biomass energy. It can be grown and burned for fuel. Another large source is waste, which can come from landfills (garbage) or the waste from manufacturing. Some cars now run on a biofuel called ethanol, which is created from crops. Ethanol can be mixed with gasoline and used in cars.

A landfill is full of stored energy.

Biomass energy suffers from the same major problem as fossil fuels: it must be burned and can be harmful to the environment. Still, it is considered less polluting than fossil fuels. It can help reduce our use of other non-renewable energy sources.

CHAPTER SEVEN

ENERGY CONSERVATION

In 1900, there were about 1.6 billion people on Earth. Today, there are more than 6 billion. Each of these people will use energy. We must find ways to meet the demand.

Power plants create pollution.

It is easy to say that we should produce more and more energy, but many sources just won't last forever. Renewable sources cannot meet the demand. To make matters worse, using more energy will mean creating more pollution.

There are only two possible solutions. We can either find new energy sources, or conserve energy. **Conservation** is the wise use of the resources we already have.

Conservation and You

A lot of our energy resources go into producing electricity. You can help conserve electricity with the flip of a switch! The simplest thing you can do to conserve electricity is to turn things off. Turning off lights that aren't needed or televisions no one is watching can save lots of energy.

One of the biggest consumers of electricity in our homes is air conditioning. Try to use it only when it's really hot outside. Turn it off at night when the temperatures drop, or better yet, see if you can get by with just a plain old electric fan.

Running an electric fan can save you energy.

When your family goes shopping for major appliances, ask them to buy appliances that are energy efficient, which means they use less electricity. Most appliances today have a sticker that shows how much energy they use. Choosing ones that are energy efficient not only saves energy, but also saves money because of lower electric bills.

Conserving Heat

Most of the heat we use in our homes goes to heating the home itself or creating hot water. There are many ways to conserve both heat and hot water.

Adjusting your home's thermostat a few degrees lower can save a lot of energy over a long winter. An even better way to conserve is to keep the heat you do use in your house and keep the cold air out. A lot of heat escapes through doors and windows—even tiny leaks can let a lot of cold air in. While it is expensive to replace doors and windows, insulating them is much cheaper and will save money in the long run.

Weather stripping can protect your windows and doors from air leaks.

To save hot water, take shorter showers and baths. Putting insulation on your boiler saves energy by protecting the hot water from the cold air around it.

If your family is shopping for appliances that use hot water, such as a new hot water heater, dishwasher, or clothes washer, suggest buying ones that use less energy and hot water.

Conserving Oil (Petroleum)

Many homes are heated by oil, so you can begin to conserve oil by saving heat. Another major use of petroleum is in transportation. Petroleum is turned into the gasoline that powers our motor vehicles.

The easiest way to conserve oil is to walk! If you can't get to your destination on foot, consider other choices, such as bikes, buses, trains or carpooling.

If your family is considering buying a new car, you can help by encouraging them to buy one that gets good gas mileage. Using less gas means a car may end up costing less over the life of the vehicle, especially if your family drives a lot.

Trolleys are a good way to conserve oil.

Recycling

Earlier on, we learned that about a third of the energy in the United States is used to make the things we buy. That's a tremendous amount of energy! It takes a lot less energy to reuse existing materials than it does to make new ones, so it makes sense to recycle.

Recycling is the process of treating materials so that they can be reused. These materials include newspapers, plastic and glass bottles, and aluminum cans.

Newspapers are recyclable.

Much of the material that can be recycled today carries the international recycling symbol, which is three arrows chasing each other in a triangle. When you see this symbol, you'll know that you can safely recycle that material.

Many places are now recycling computers, stereos, TVs, and other electronic devices that used to be placed in landfills. The metal and plastic on these appliances can be reused. Even the ink cartridge on your printer can be recycled easily these days by bringing it in to a store.

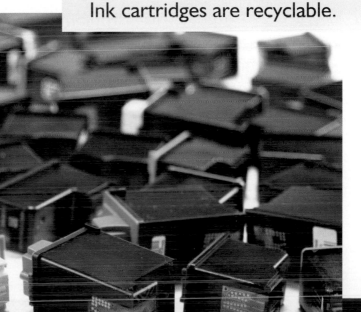

Ink cartridges are recyclable.

10 Easy Ways to Can Save Energy

You're just a kid! You can't help save energy, right? WRONG! There are many ways each and every one of us can help save energy every day. Here's a brief list of some easy ways to cut energy use. See how many others you can think of!

1. Wash the dishes by hand instead of using the dishwasher, saving electricity and hot water.
2. Keep the refrigerator door closed! Keeping the door open even for a short time allows a lot of cold air to escape.
3. Unplug cell phones, computers, and even TVs when they aren't needed. They all use energy, even when they are turned off!
4. Reuse supermarket bags. These bags are made of paper (from wood) or plastic (from petroleum).
5. Ride your bike instead of asking someone to drive you to nearby places.
6. Close the curtains. This can help keep warm air in your house in the winter, and prevent hot air from getting inside in the summer.
7. Use a fan instead of an air conditioner.
8. Hang laundry outside to dry instead of using a clothes dryer.
9. Start a recycling drive at your school. Discuss with your teachers how you can recycle all the paper you use.
10. Help educate others about saving energy. The more people you can get to join you, the more energy you'll help save!

CHAPTER EIGHT

THE FUTURE OF ENERGY

Will there be enough energy to last us into the future? Can we expect to have all the energy we need? The answers to these questions will depend on how wisely we use the non-renewable resources we have, and how we can improve or find new sources of renewable energy.

Solar energy may help us meet our increasing energy demands. The amount of solar energy that reaches the Earth in an hour is greater than the energy we use in a year! As solar technology improves we may be able to harness much more of that renewable energy source.

One promising technology is hydrogen fuel cells. These cells can be used to power anything from small devices such as cell phones to larger things such as automobiles. Right now, fuel cells are expensive to make. If the cost comes down, fuel cells may help us meet our future energy needs.

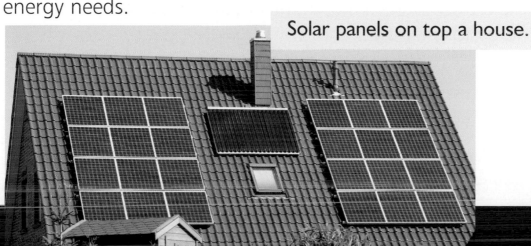

Solar panels on top a house.

Another technology that is changing our energy use right now is the hybrid automobile. The word hybrid means that something comes from more than one source. In the case of cars, the hybrid engine uses both gasoline and electric energy. It converts the braking power of the car into electric energy to charge the batteries.

A hybrid car.

Whatever the future holds, it's clear that we need to do three things to make sure we have enough energy. First, we must make wise use of our non-renewable resources. Next, we must conserve energy whenever we can. Finally, we must look to new technologies to help us meet our future demands.

If we do these things today, there will be plenty of energy for many years to come.

Questions to Consider

1. What is the difference between kinetic and potential energy? Give an example of how one type can be turned into the other.

2. What might the future be like if we fail to come up with ways to meet our increasing demand for energy?

3. If you were president, what steps might you take to reduce the pollution caused by burning fossil fuels?

Websites to Visit

http://www.cia.doe.gov/kids/index.html
http://epa.gov/climatechange/kids/index.html
http://www.energyquest.ca.gov/

Further Reading

Saunders, Nigel and Steven Chapman. *Renewable Energy*. Raintree, 2005.

VanCleave, Janice. *Energy for Every Kid: Easy Activities That Make Learning Science Fun*. Joosey-Bass, 2005.

Wheeler, Jill C. *Everyday Conservation (Eye on Energy)*. Checkerboard Books, 2007.

GLOSSARY

biomass energy (BI-oh-mass) — plant material and animal waste burned as fuel

chemical energy (KHEM-eh-kul) — the energy released through a chemical reaction

conservation (con-sur-VAY-shun) — the wise use of the resources we already have

electrical energy (e-LEC-trih-kul) — the movement of electrons through a conductor

energy (EN ur gee) — the ability to do work

fossil fuels (FOSS-ul) — fuels that come from dead organisms. They include coal, oil, and natural gas

geothermal energy (jee-oh-THUR-mal) — energy that comes from the Earth in the form of water or steam

heat (HEET) **energy** — the movement of energy from one object to another

hydropower (HI-dro-pow-er) — energy captured from the movement of water

kinetic energy (ki-NET-ik) — the energy of movement

Law of Conservation of Energy (con-sur-VAY-shun) — states that energy can neither be created nor destroyed

non-renewable energy (NON re-NYOO-a-bull) — energy that we will run out of someday

nuclear energy (NOO-klee-er) — the potential energy stored in the nucleus of an atom

potential energy (po-TEN-shul) — stored energy

recycling (ree-SIGH-kull-ing) — the process of treating materials so that they can be reused

renewable energy (re-NYOO-a-bull) — energy that can be used over and over, without running out

solar energy (SO ler) — energy that comes from the sun

thermal energy (THUR-mul) — see heat energy

turbine (TUR-byne) — an engine that gets its energy from the pressure of wind, air, water, or some other energy source

wind power (WIND)— energy captured from the movement of the wind

work (WURK) — the ability to make an object move in some way

INDEX

About the Author

Tim Clifford is an education writer and an author of several children's books. He is a teacher who lives and works in New York City.